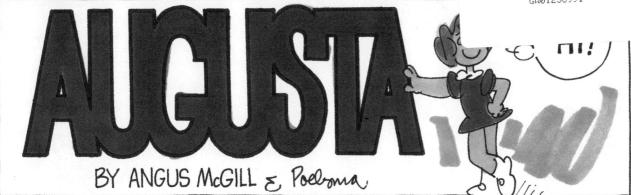

Published by Harmsworth Publications Ltd. for
and on behalf of Associated Newspapers plc.

© 1989 Associated Newspapers plc.

ISBN 0 85144 522 3

Printed and bound by Richard Clay Ltd. Bungay, Suffolk

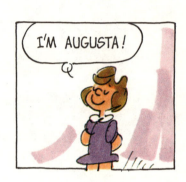

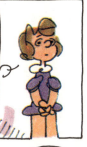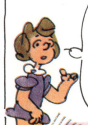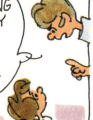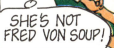

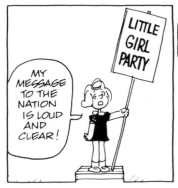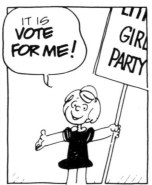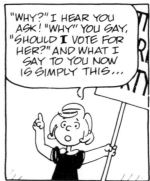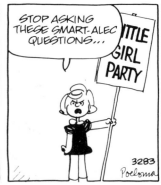
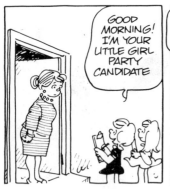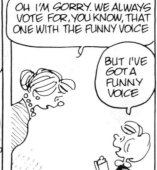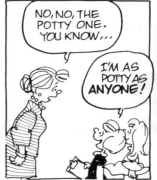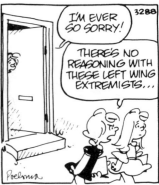

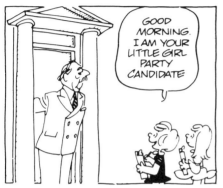
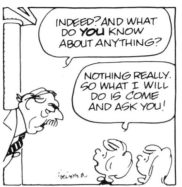
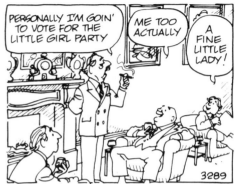
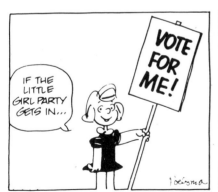
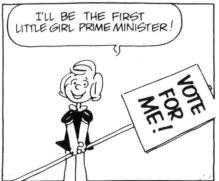
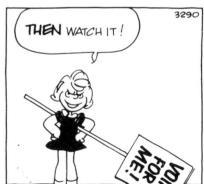

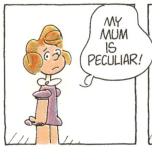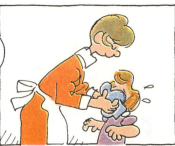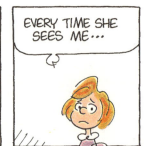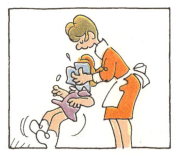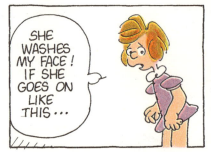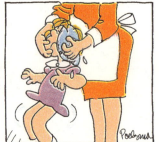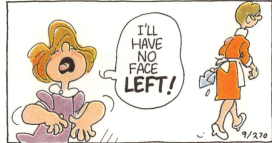

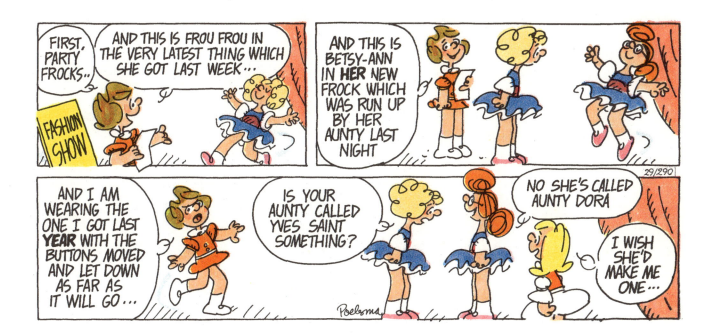

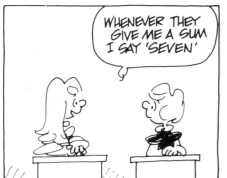
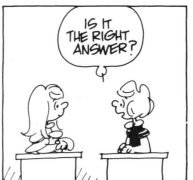
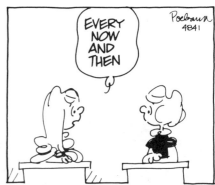
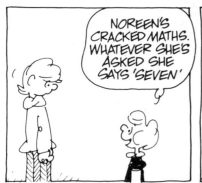
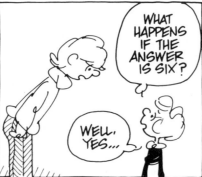
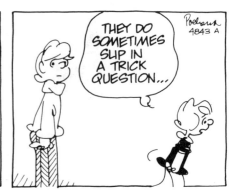

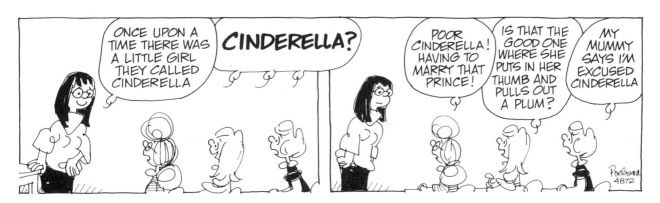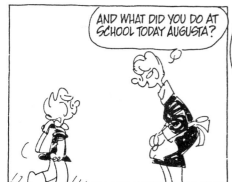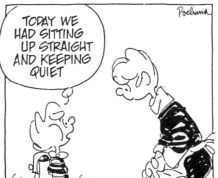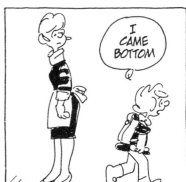

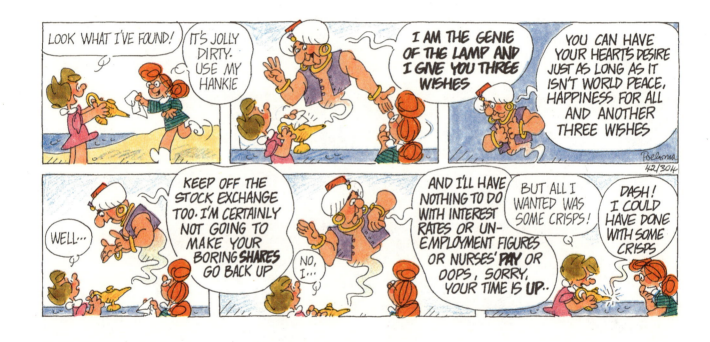

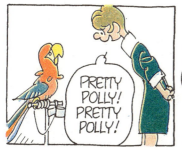
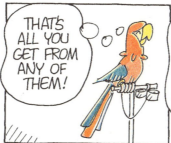
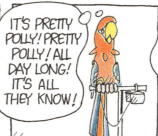
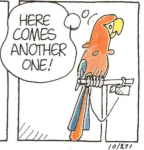
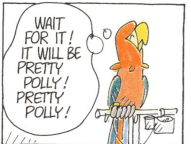
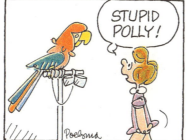
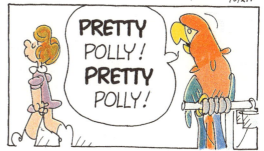

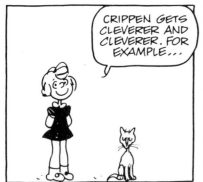
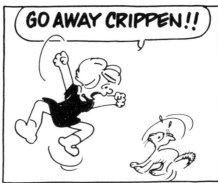
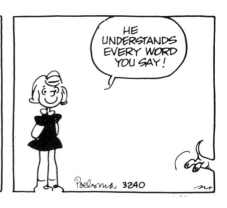
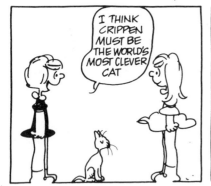
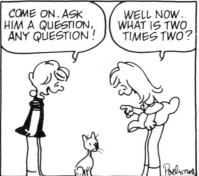
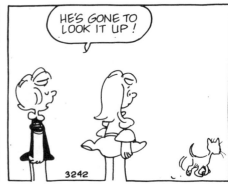

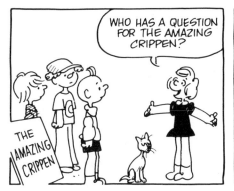
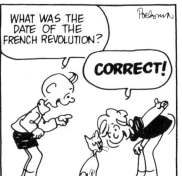
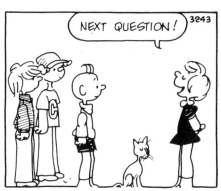
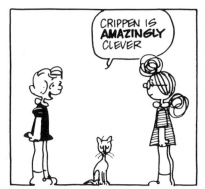
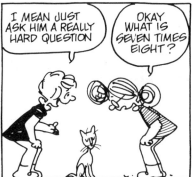
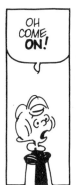
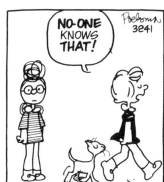

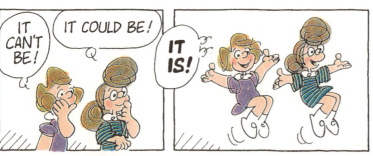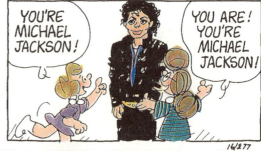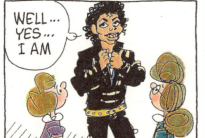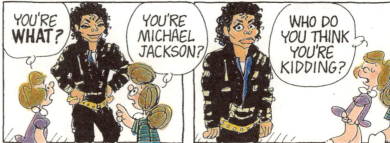

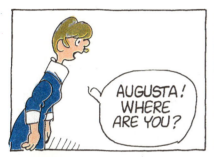
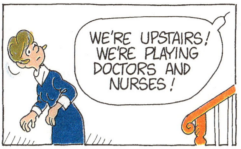
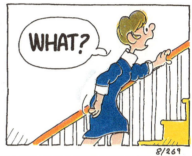
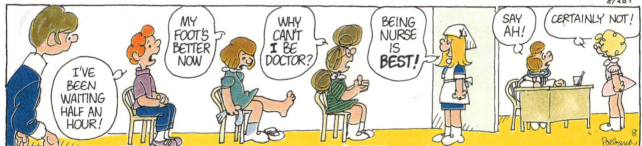

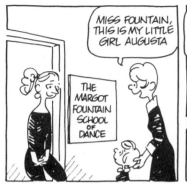
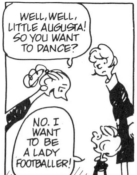
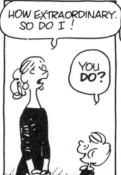
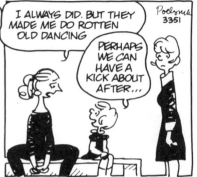
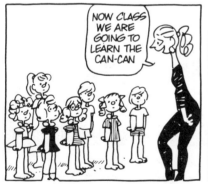
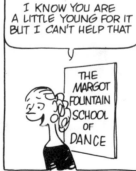
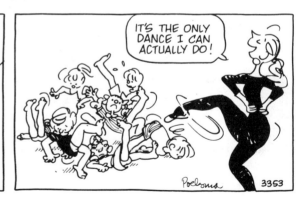

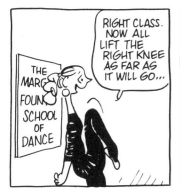
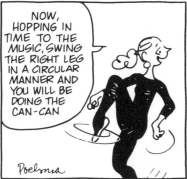
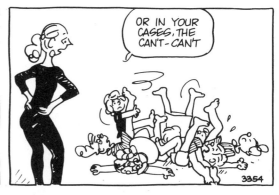
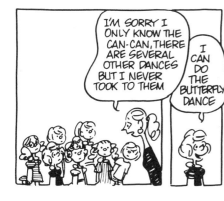
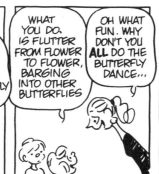
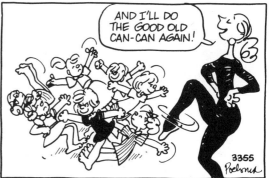

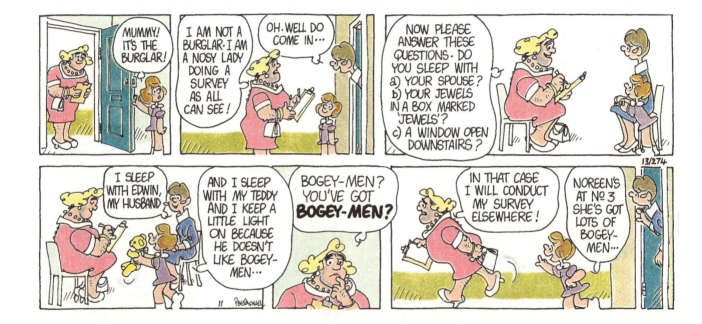

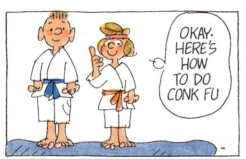
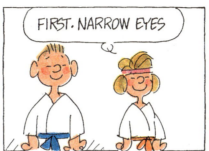
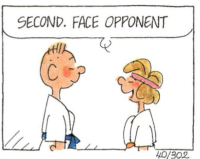
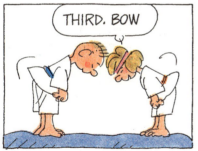
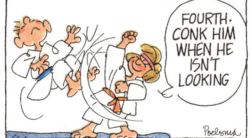
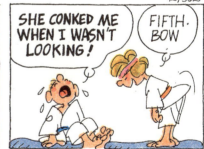

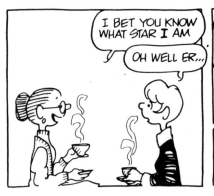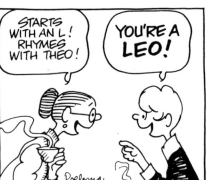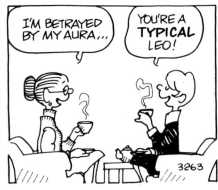
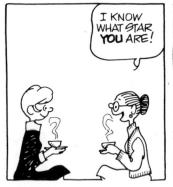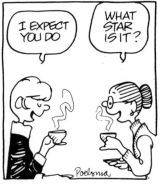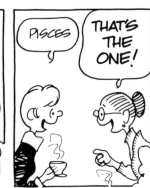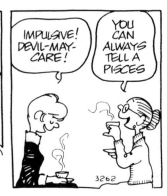

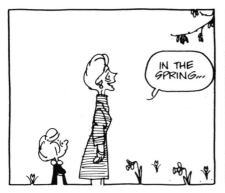
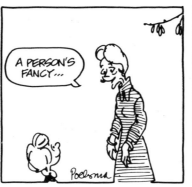
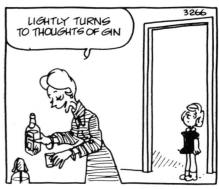
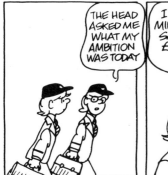
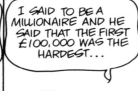
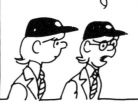
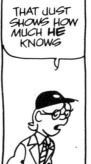
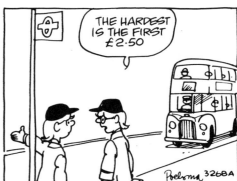

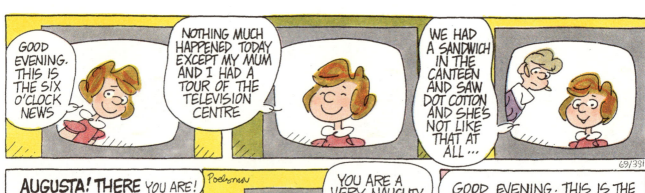
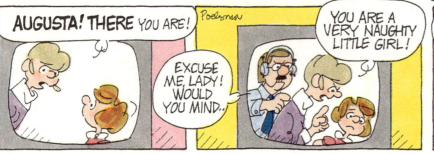
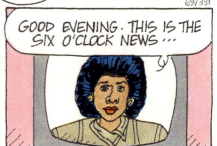

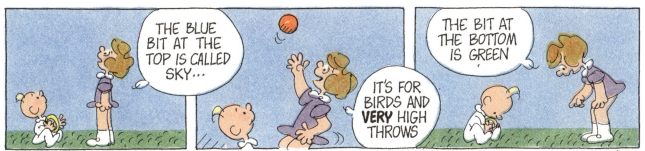

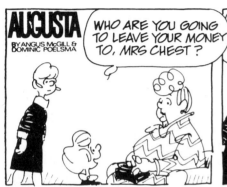
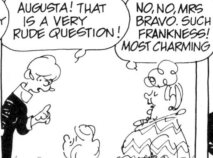
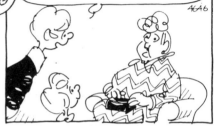
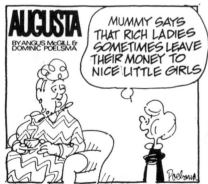
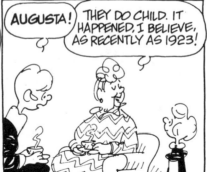
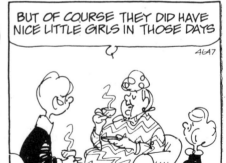

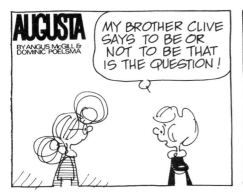
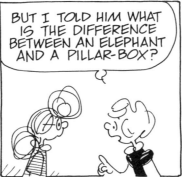
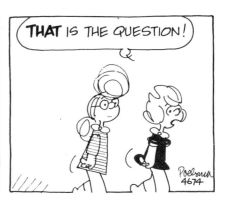
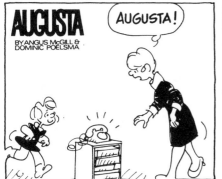
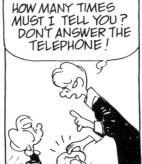
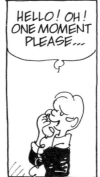
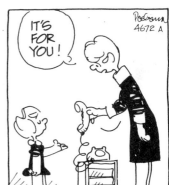

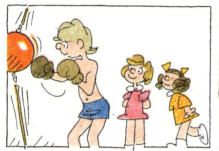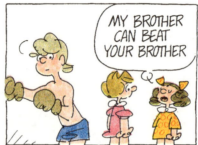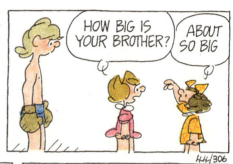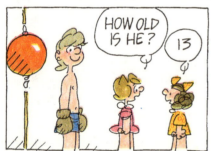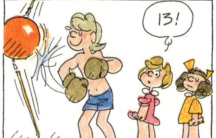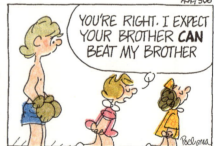

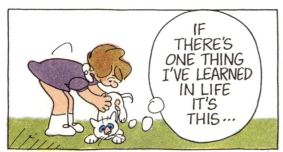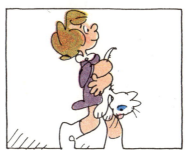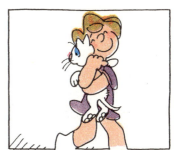
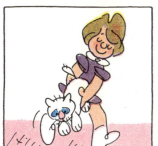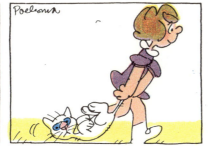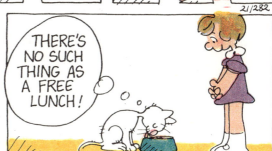

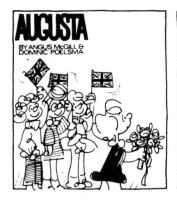
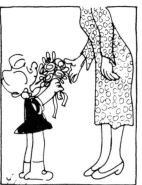
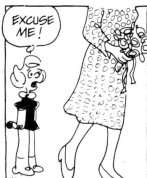
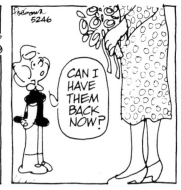
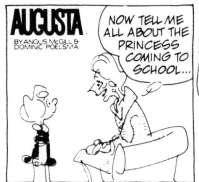
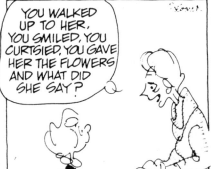
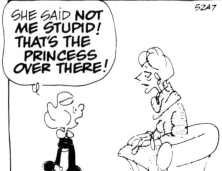

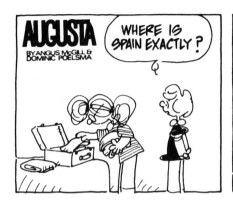
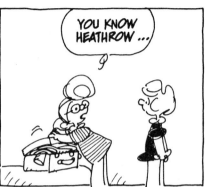
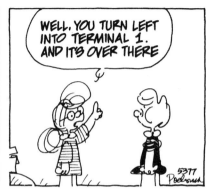
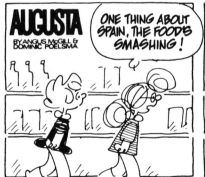
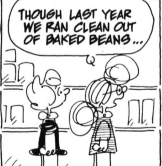
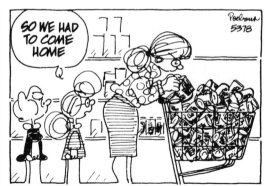

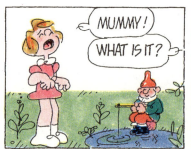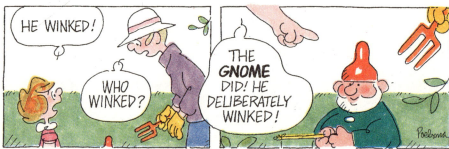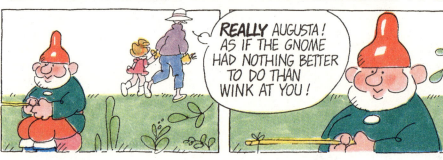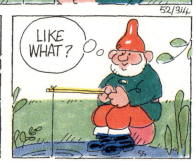

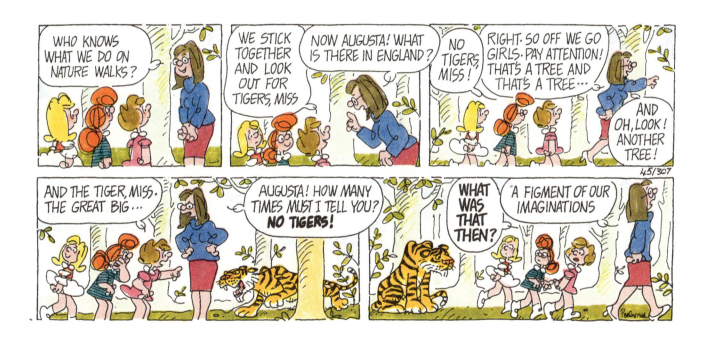

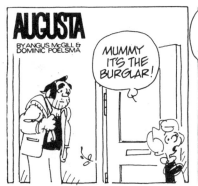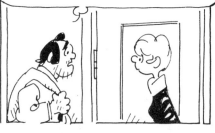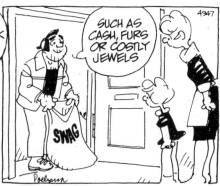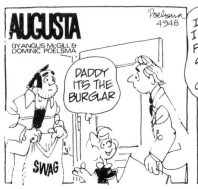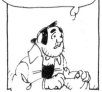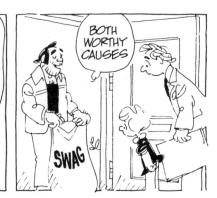

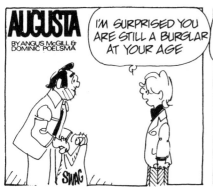
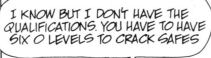
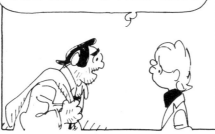
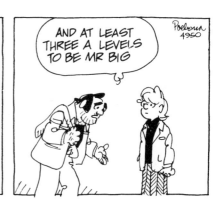
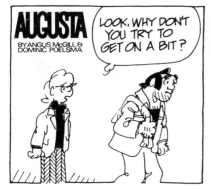
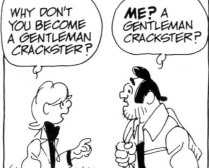
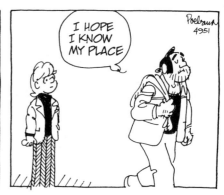

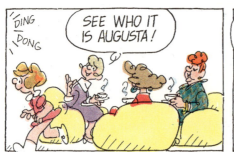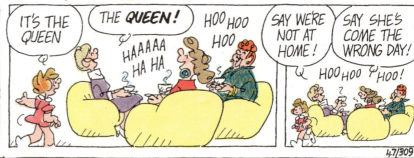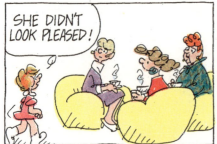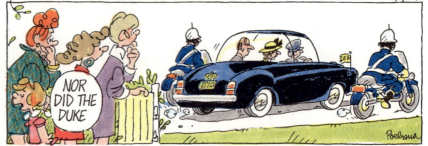

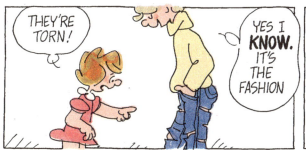
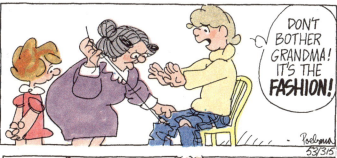
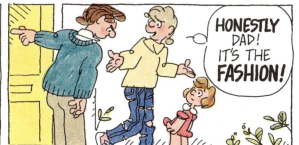
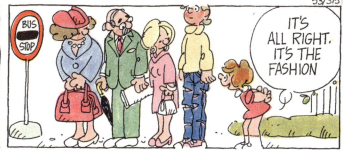

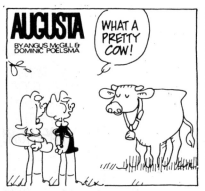
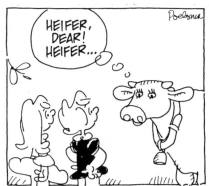
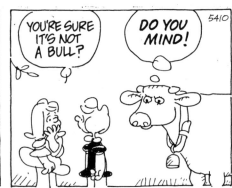
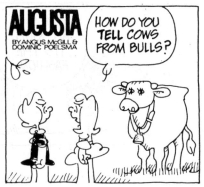
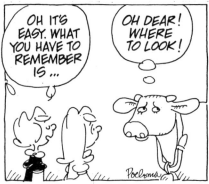
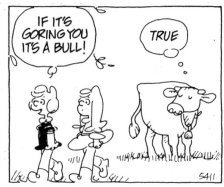

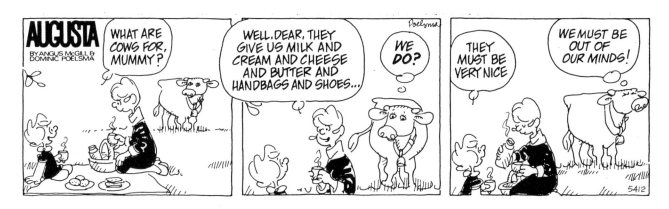
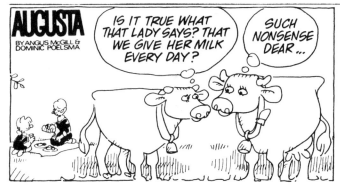
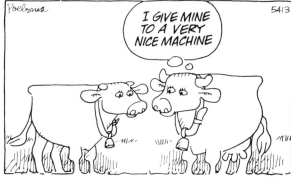

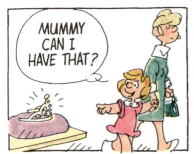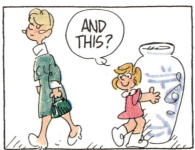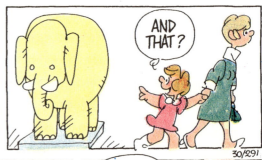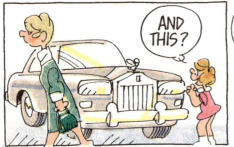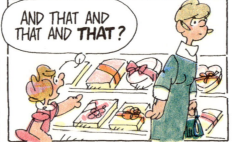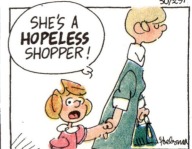

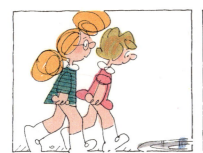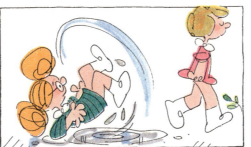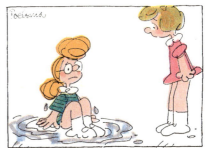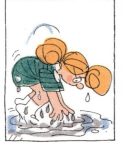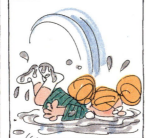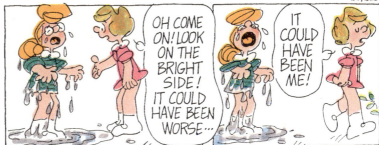

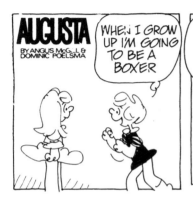
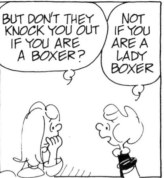
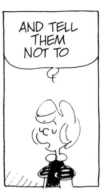
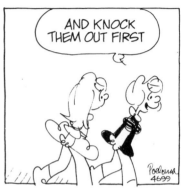
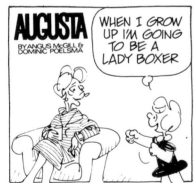
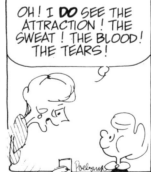
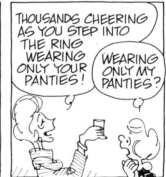
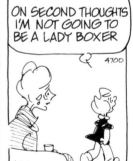

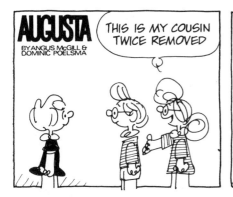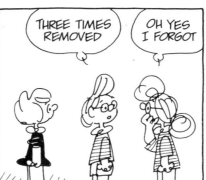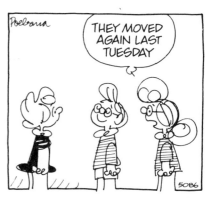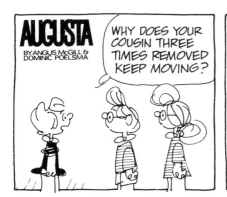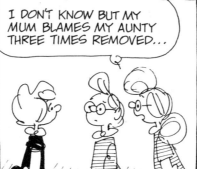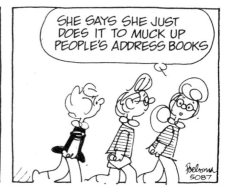

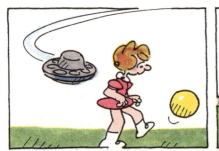
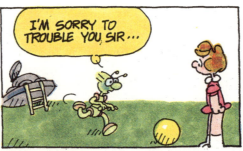
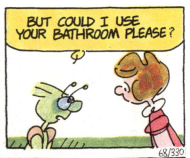
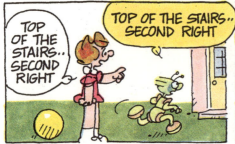
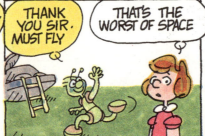
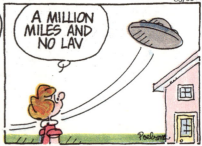

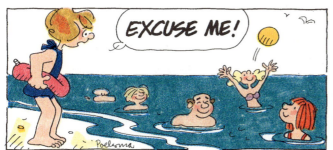
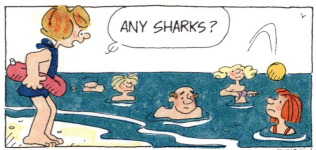
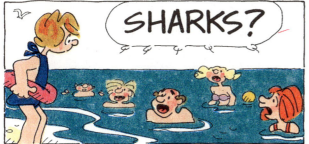
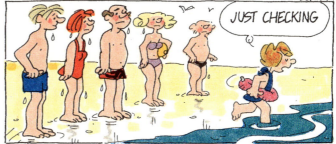

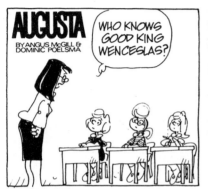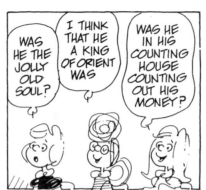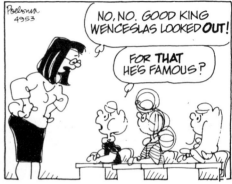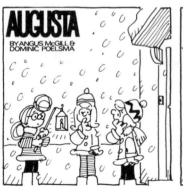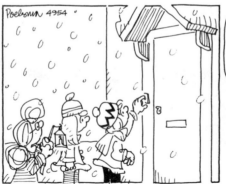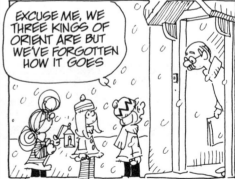

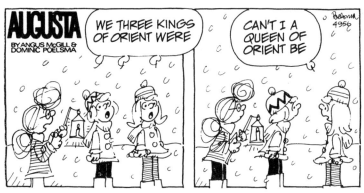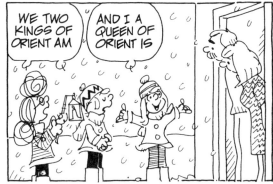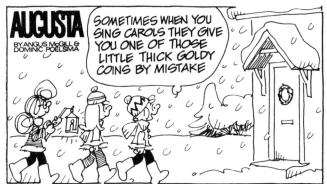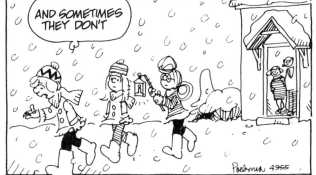

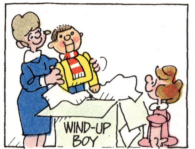 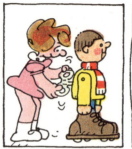 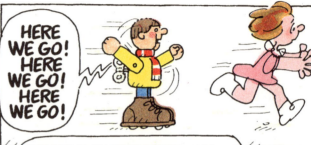
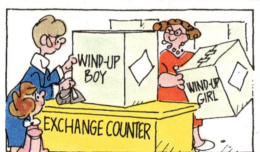 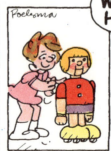 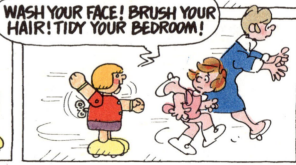

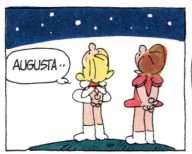
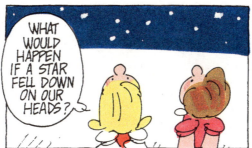
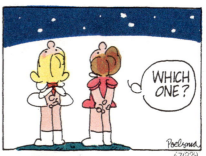
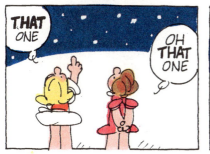
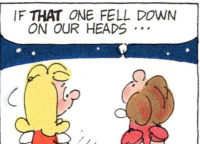
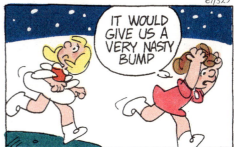

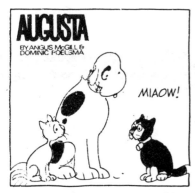
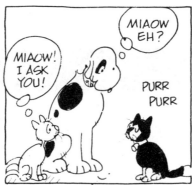
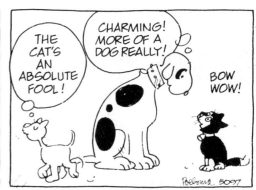
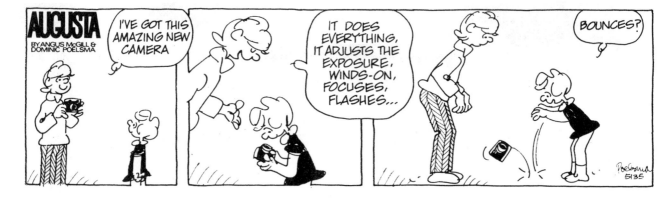

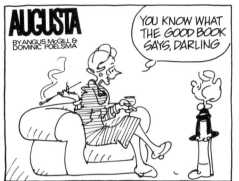
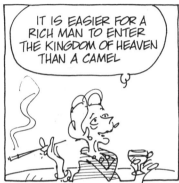
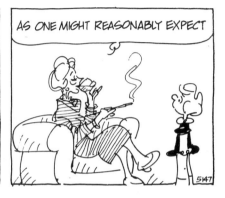
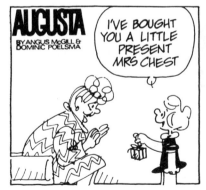
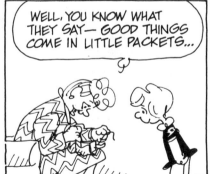
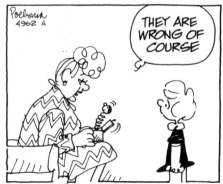

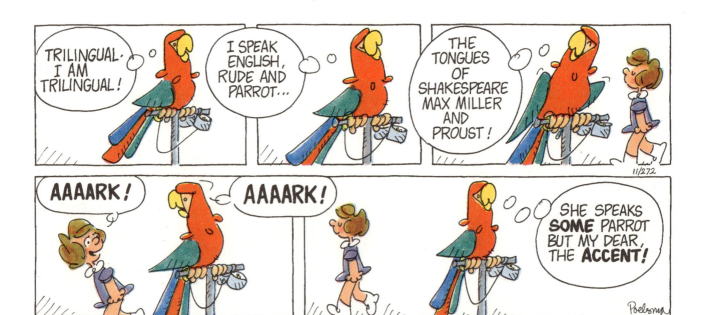

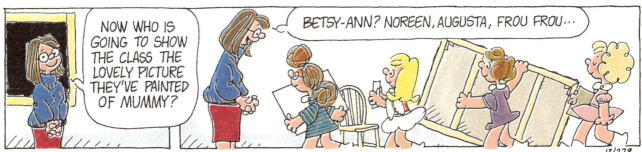
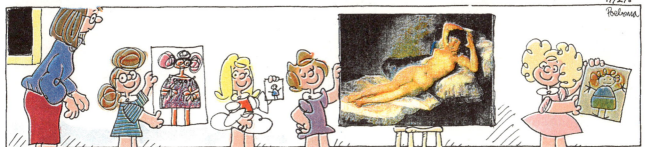

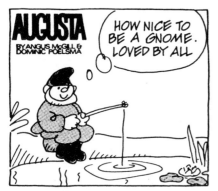
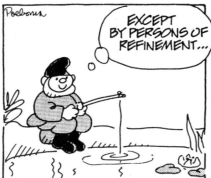
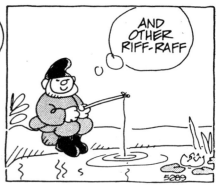
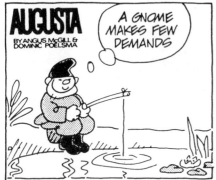
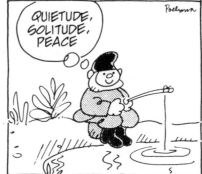
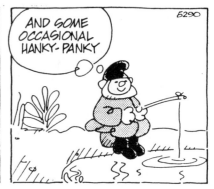

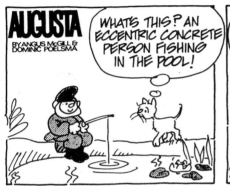
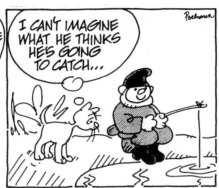
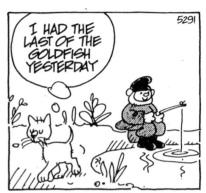
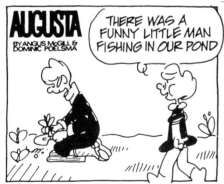
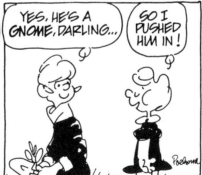
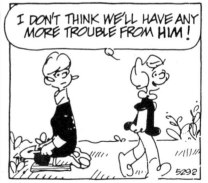

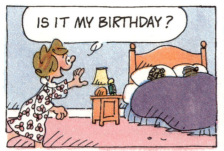
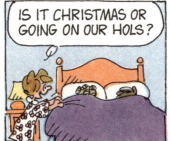
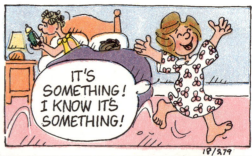
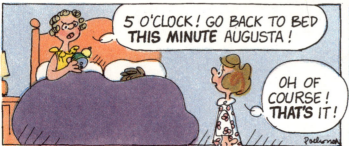
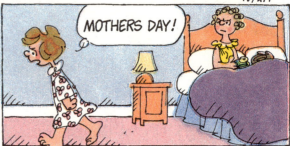

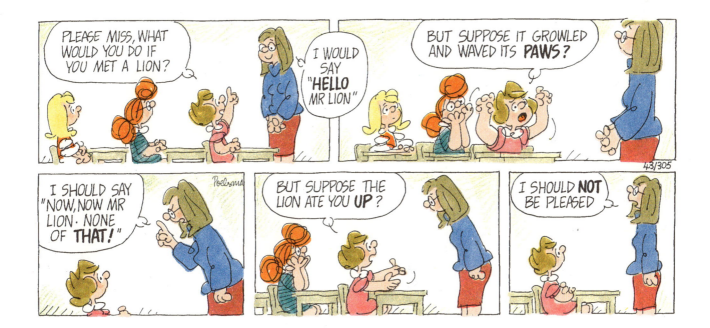

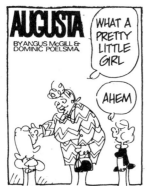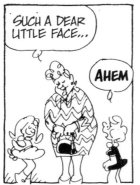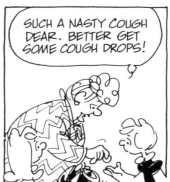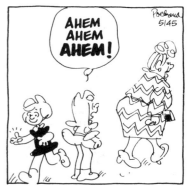
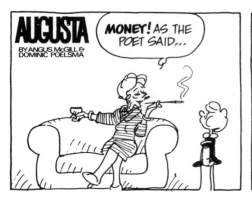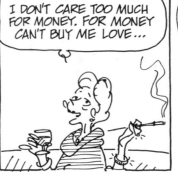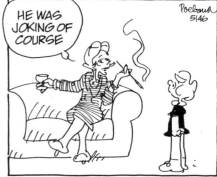

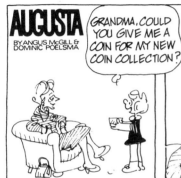
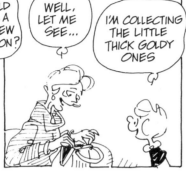
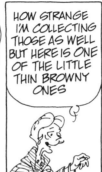
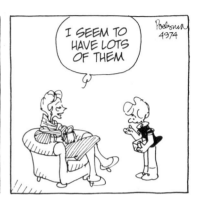
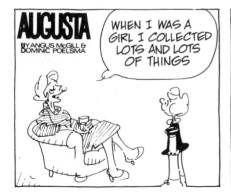
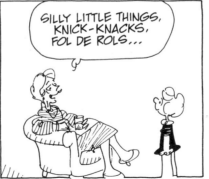
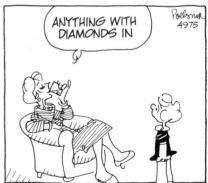

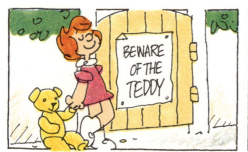
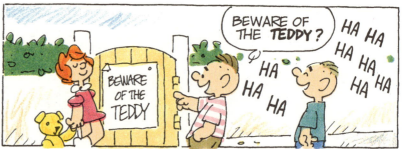
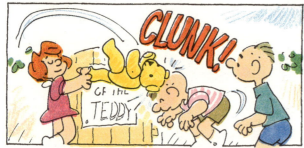
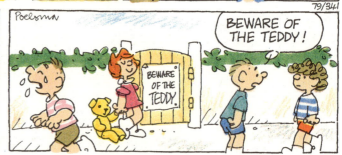

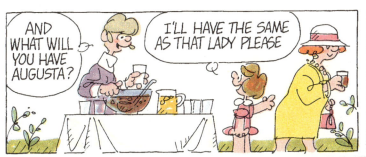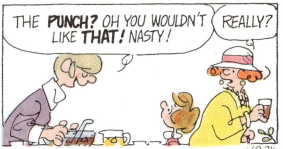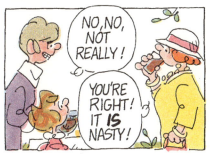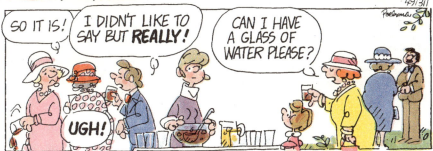

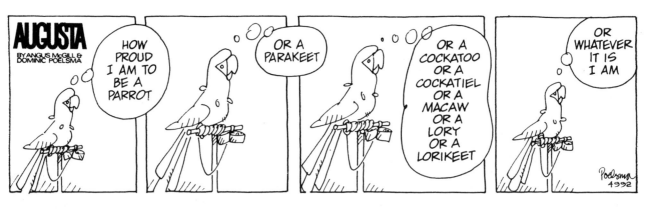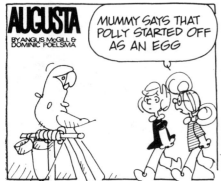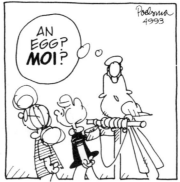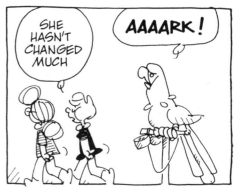

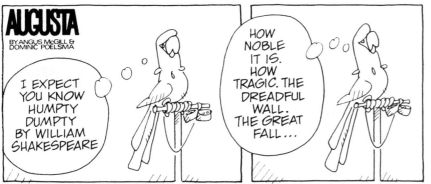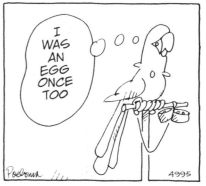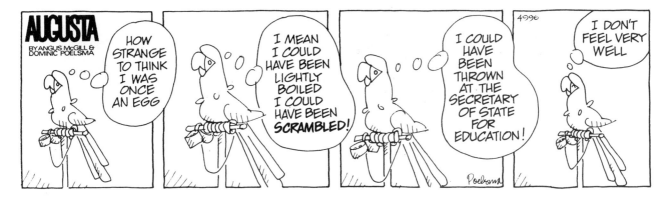

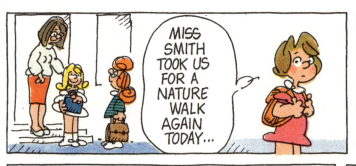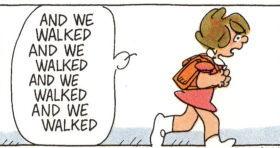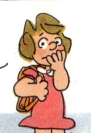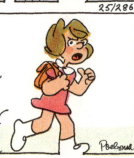

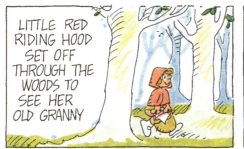
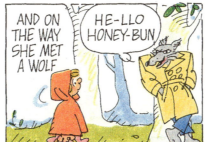
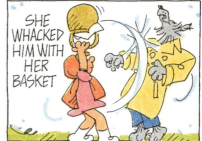
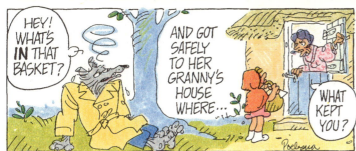
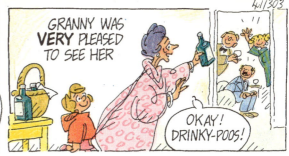

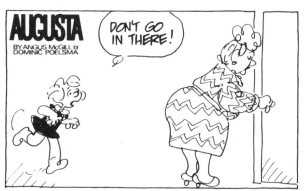
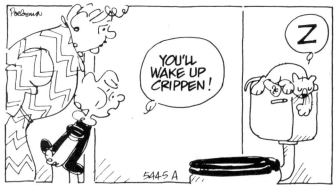
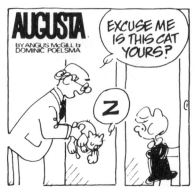
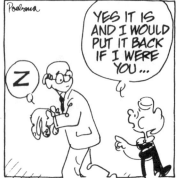
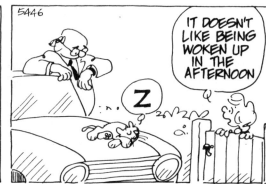

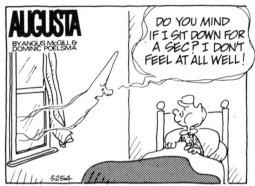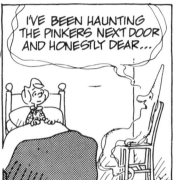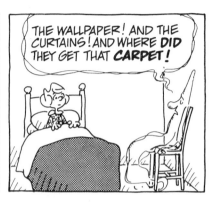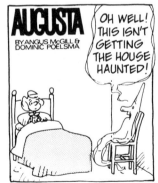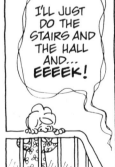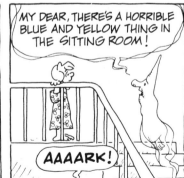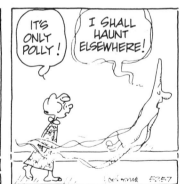

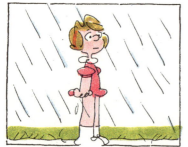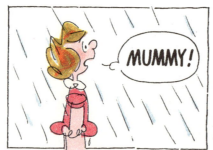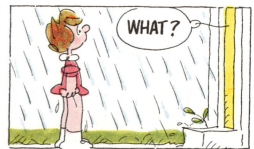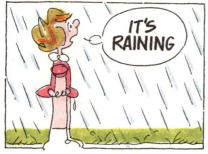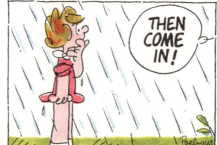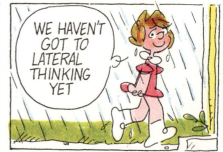

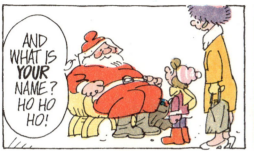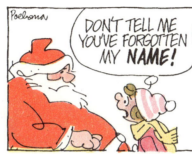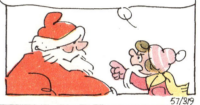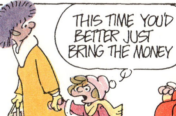

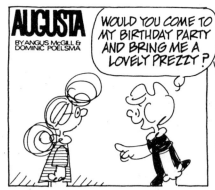
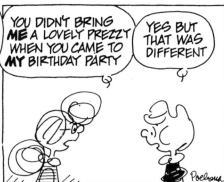
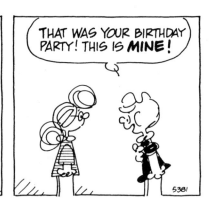
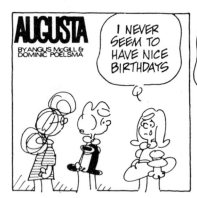
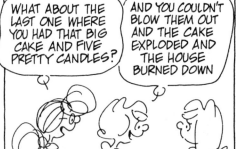
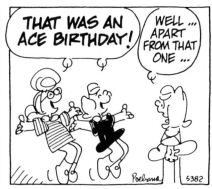

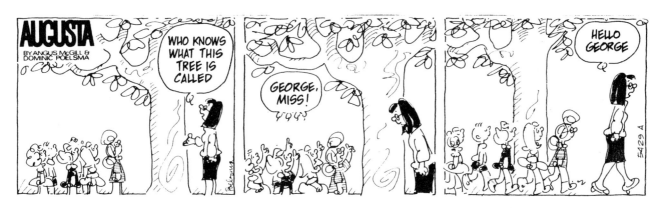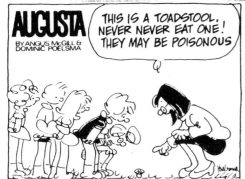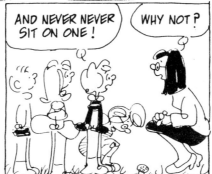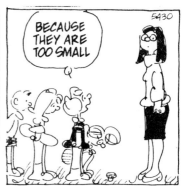

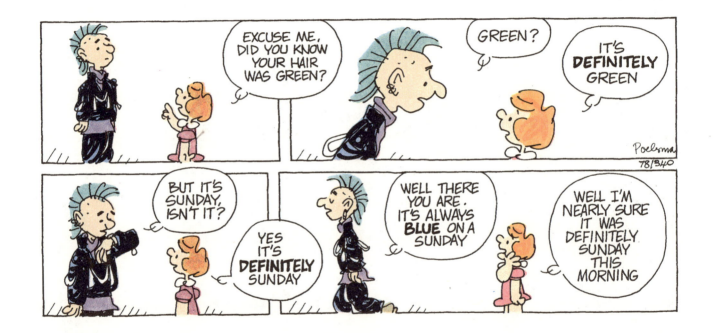

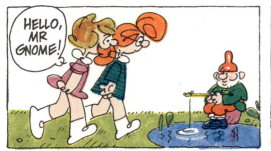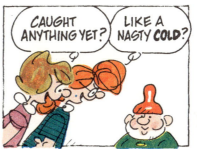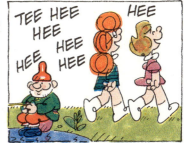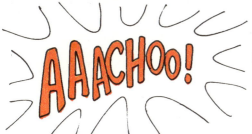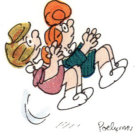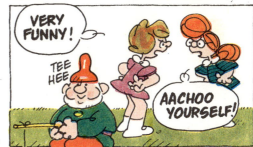

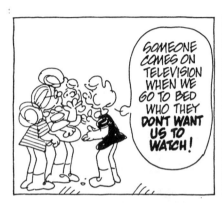
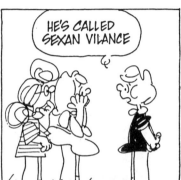
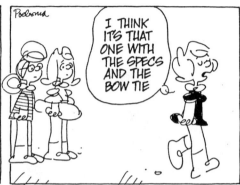
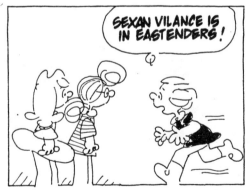
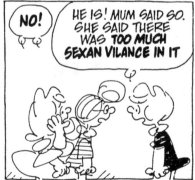
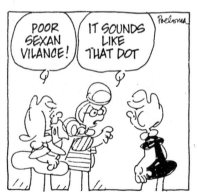

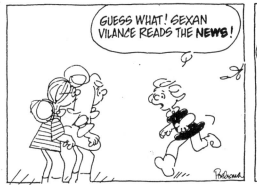
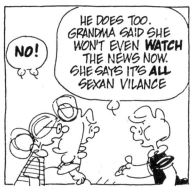
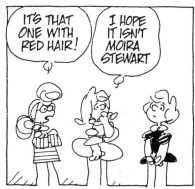
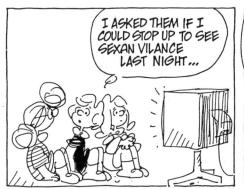
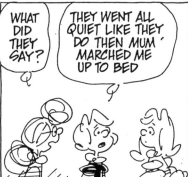
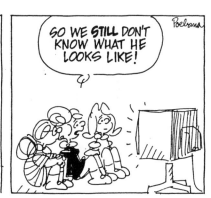

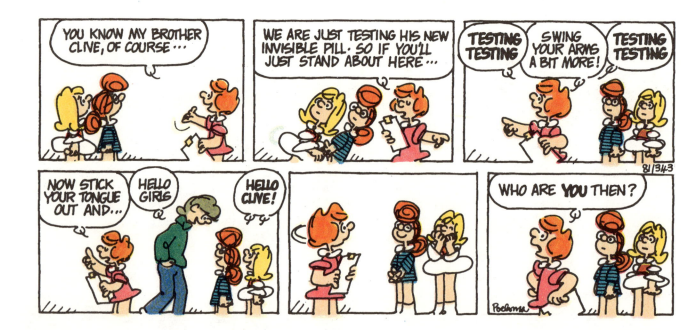

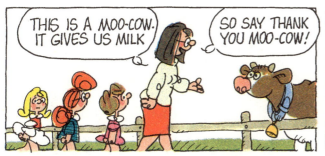
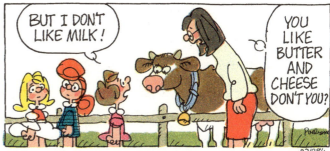
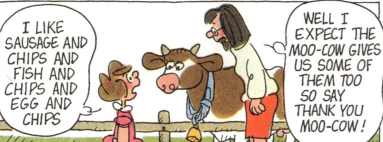
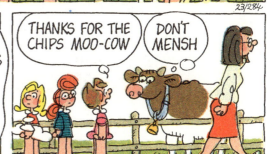

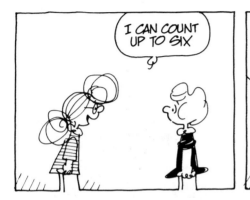
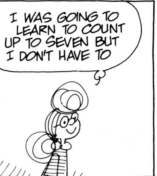
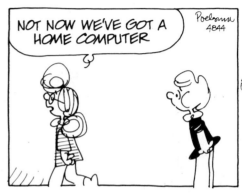
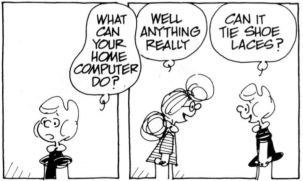
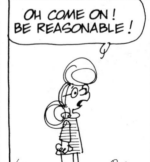
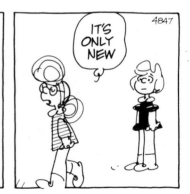

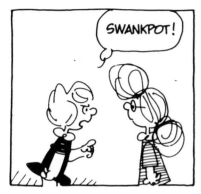
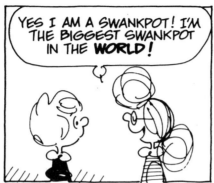
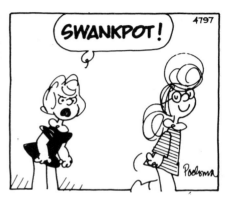
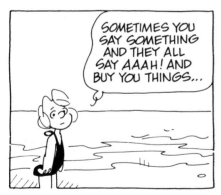
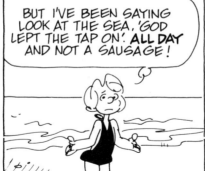
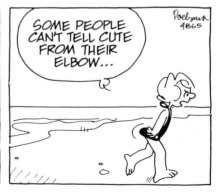

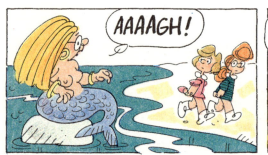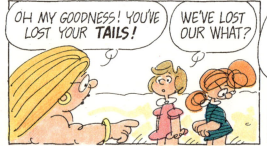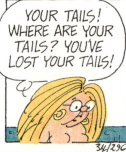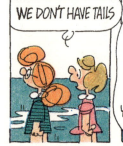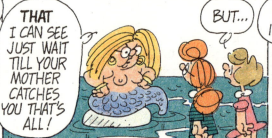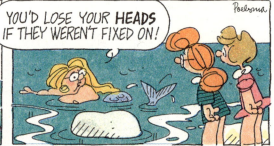

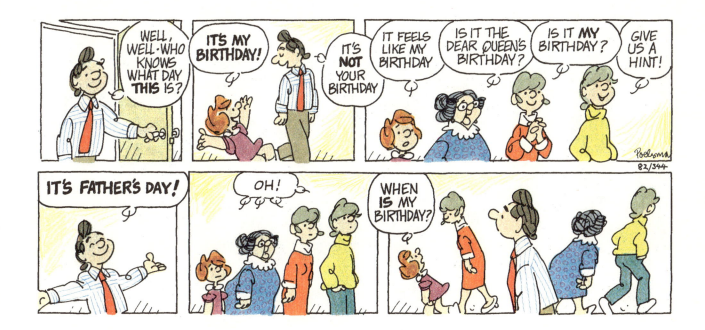

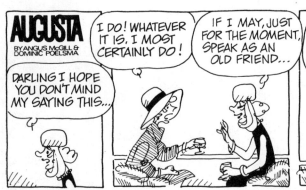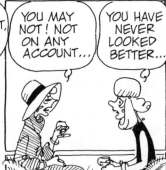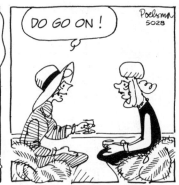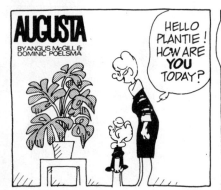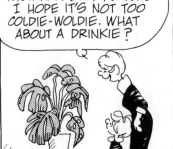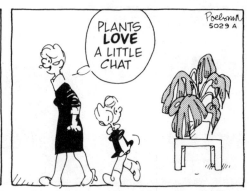